# The Turnaround:

## Amazing Stories of Success

## from Ordinary People

## Who Turned Their Dream Ideas

## into Thriving Businesses

By Boomy Tokan

The Turnaround:  Amazing Stories of Success from Ordinary
People Who Turned Their Dream Ideas  into Thriving Businesses

Copyright © 2013 Boomy Tokan

# Content

# Free Bonus ⋯

FREE Bonus –

"How To Start Your Own Business In 30 Days"

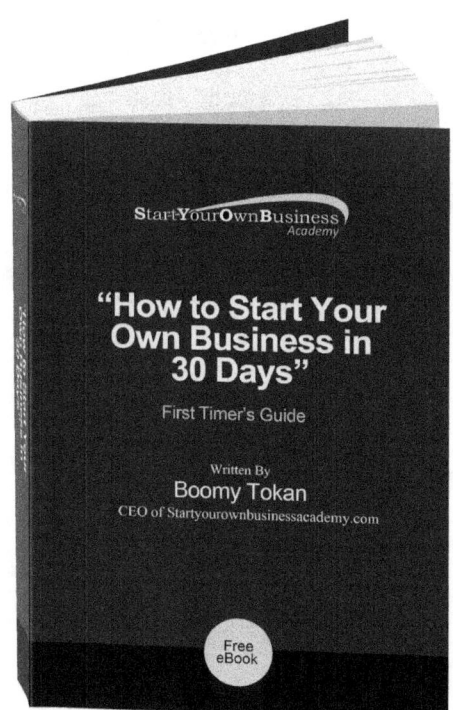

Hey … If you would like to learn how to start and run a "High Performance" business; then download this FREE guide.  It will also show you how to start making money from your business within 30 Days! **Available only for a Limited Period.**

Click this link:

"How To Start Your Own Business In 30 Days"

Or Copy and paste in your browser:

http://startyourownbusinessacademy.com/free-bonus-download/

Enjoy

# Introduction

My story.

My own writing career began four years ago. I wrote a forty-page book and another shorter one. Then I began considering how I might possibly start selling the book. I approached a publisher who expressed an interest but asked me to pay $6,000 (£4,000) for the privilege of having my book on paper. At the time, I did not have the money for such a venture, plus the thought of paying someone to print/promote my book just did not sit well with me. I was under the impression that the publishers paid me!

After this episode, I left the books on my hard-disk for another three years. Then just out of the blue something happened that changed my story. Kemi, my neighbor, told me one morning she was meeting a friend who was selling books online. Apparently it cost her nothing to set up the process and hundreds of books were sold monthly. My ears pricked and I asked her if I could join the meeting. She said no problem.

That was when I meet Mavis. She came that afternoon and spoke to us about the opportunity of publishing on Kindle. "Kindle, what is that?" I asked. She took us through the process and that same month I started selling books on Amazon KDP (Kindle Direct Publishing).

More importantly Mavis became my "Kindle Mentor" At one point I was speaking to her every morning and learning the ropes! On one of those occasions she told me I needed to start publishing stories. The idea of telling other peoples stories just did not resonate with me. But when Mavis spoke I listened and considered what she said even if I didn't like it. I have a lot of respect for her on many levels. So I parked the idea somewhere in my mind even though I was not excited about it.

Seven months later I read a book by "Rachel," a web expert, where she spoke about writing stories. The bells began ringing in my mind. I remembered what Mavis had previously said and I decided to collect stories of how people started in business!

Now, I don't know what I expected but whatever it was, the stories you are about to read in this book are some of the most amazing stories in the world! Honestly, whenever I started reading a story, I just could not stop until I finished. The stories in this book made me say, "Wow," "Oh My GOD," and "My Goodness," all at the same time. Some made me want to cry! Some made me quiet and numb. Many made me so excited I wanted to scream "Hallelujah!" One thing is for sure – when you read these stories, your life will not remain the same. You will be inspired and instructed to make life-changing decisions no matter what hardships, difficulties, or obstacles you are facing right now.

Get ready to hear from some of the most amazing men and women in the world as they share their true life stories of how they started their own businesses and turned their lives around!

# A Mother Of Four Turned $65 Into A Global Business

*The Teri Gaults Turnaround Story*

The Grocery Game

www.TheGroceryGame.com

I started a new life on my 40th birthday… Since I was in my late teens, I had been an actress in TV and film. After that, for eleven years, I worked as a professional singer and recording artist. I had nine first ballot GRAMMY nominations as a "boy soprano" in early renaissance, and remain an active member of NARAS and still attend the Grammys and NARAS events. I also recorded and performed as a jazz ensemble singer. My life was entertainment and music.

Until… By the mid-90s, the entertainment business was slowing down for me and my husband, who was also in the film business. We resorted to selling everything that wasn't nailed down to pay our rent and put food on the table.

During those trying years, we did everything we could to survive, which included re-discovering something I was passionate about since childhood… saving with coupons! I was rolling $35 a week to feed our family of four, and became an expert at grocery savings. In February of 2000, on my 40th birthday, I rolled $65 in coins and marched into city hall to buy my business license for my new website that I had built to help others save like me. At times, having given up music, it really did feel like death of a dream, but this was a new dream, and I gave it my all, and gave up everything for it…

9

I worked day and night in my bedroom/office putting my money-saving lists for my local stores on the website. I had found my true purpose, as I read countless emails from those who had used my list and told me their stories of how life changing it was to be able to feed their families well, and for less. In February of 2003, we expanded into 26 states through franchising.

Now, www.TheGroceryGame.com is offering over 200 lists in all 50 states and 7 foreign countries. In September of 2010, we launched the only one of its kind in the world, comparison-shopping website with un-advertised sales. Grocery Gamers report average savings of $514 a month for a family of four, or about $6,000 a year in savings! Challenges: The most obvious obstacle in tackling this brainstorm was that I had never seen the internet, plus by nature I am extremely techno phobic. I don't even watch TV when I'm home alone, because the multiple remote controls intimidate me!

Nevertheless, with no money to invest I did everything on a shoestring, which meant I had to build my first website myself. The website was free for the first three months, so I had to move quickly to start making money before I had a new bill that I wouldn't be able to pay. I discovered the website tech support guys were available in the wee hours of the night and morning. So for three weeks, I stayed up all night, and with their free help was able to build a nice website that would immediately begin to draw visitors. My "office" was cramped in my bedroom, between my side of the bed and the wall.

Boxes and filing cabinets lined the walls of the bedroom, and closets were mostly filled with everything but clothes. I worked seven days a week, twenty-hour days, and even pulled many "all-nighters." All because I was still holding down some part-time jobs, and with my new business, there were no hours left to the day. My husband stepped into "Mr. Mom" roles and everything else that kept the home fires burning. When exhausted to the point of giving up, his constant encouragement re-fueled me to carry on. He always promised my efforts would snow-ball, and they did.

But I still wanted and needed to be a mom. So I found ways to keep my mom role in the home. In that first few years, I nearly killed myself, because a new business with a family can take its toll. It's very important to know your physical limitations.

I learned the hard way. I ended up in the hospital, overworked and with a stress-induced illness. Once out of that scary spot, I found out that I could still work full speed ahead on the business, but I had to find balance. Time spent on the business could not be pruned back. So this only meant I had to prune outside obligations, activities and even some relationships. I could no longer be room mom or team mom, or volunteer at the food pantry, and more. After "pruning" some things down, I was closer to sanity, but clearly more had to go.

There just weren't enough hours in a day or week to give my business what it needed, and be the mother that I wanted to be for my kids. So I learned that I could not have outside activities on top of all of that. Rewards: I love the mom and pop family feeling we have in the company. Everyone works from home, some with babies on their laps. I love it that we can allow people to be flexible with scheduling, that we can communicate with each other, and help each other out. It really feels like a family.

# How A "Ha Ha" Moment Turned Into An A-List Enterprise

*The Craig Wolfe Turnaround Story*

Celebri Ducks

www.celebriDucks.com

I think I might have a fun little story for you here. I started two different successful businesses based on my passions and learned a lot of hard lessons along the way, which fortunately taught me a lot and helped me to succeed.

It might help to give you a little background first. I may have more info than you need, but I think there is definitely something here that makes me feel I might be of interest for this topic.

My company CelebriDucks does a whole line of celebrity rubber ducks that were voted one of the top 100 gifts by Entertainment Weekly. I'll post our press kit letter below. I actually started with $1000. Also, I outsource around the world so have a lot more than 25 people working on projects for me, but don't keep hundreds of people on payroll.

When I graduated college with a degree in business and religion I really had no direction. I always found that if I wasn't moved to something emotionally, that I couldn't really conceive of it as an area of serious livelihood for myself. One day, I saw an original drawing of Mickey Mouse in a store all framed up hanging on the wall...and for sale no less! I was instantly captivated by the raw energy in the animator's hand drawing.

It was one of the actual drawings that was used in a real 1930's Disney cartoon short. I had no idea you people could own these things let alone that they even existed. Ah ha!...direction! I would soon seek out where to get more of these things and thus my original business Name That Toon was born where I would buy and sell original Disney vintage animation drawings.

The company expanded and eventually I hooked up with some people and together we were going to make a presentation to Fox to market the artwork from the Simpson cartoons. As it turned out, we didn't get the contract. I was really disappointed, but knew that if I continued to follow my heart and move in the direction where I felt inspired, I would eventually be led to something even better for me. And it didn't take long for that to happen.

I was watching TV and saw The California Raisin commercials. I was amazed! The combination of top-notch clay animation with the Motown sound track and witty scenarios was absolutely captivating. To make a long story short, I contacted the studio doing the animation and ended up marketing the artwork from the commercials and cartoons featuring the raisins. So that was pretty much my business up to that point...until one day, fate again intervened.

One day, I was walking down the street and passed a storefront window for Macy's. In the window were all these old vintage Coca-Cola vending machines, old glass bottles of Coke, and other assorted memorabilia. I was dumbstruck. Honestly, it was probably the closest I ever came to having an epiphany. In an instant, I felt all the power of those old time commercials, vending machines, all the feelings of nostalgia and old time feelings of time past. I immediately went inside and worked out a deal to buy their whole window display.

Then I called Coke and told them I wanted to market the original artwork from their commercials the way Disney marketed their original animation cells from their classic cartoons. It took about a year for them to totally get what I wanted to do. They were right in the midst of the Coke Polar Bear commercials.

Part of the problem was all the animation was done via computer. So how do you get the images out of the computer onto an animation cel like a Disney was doing with their hand-painted work? I mean I'm an English-Religion major from Hobart College without a shred of business or technical training. But you know how it is…when you feel passionate about something, doors open and you connect with the right people to help you make your dreams a reality.

Eventually I figured that all out and did in fact get a contract to do this for Coke. I worked directly with the animation studio who was doing the animation on coming up with a process to make it work. Bottom, line, not only did it work, but they went on to become one of Coke's top selling art pieces at that time.

We then went on to become the largest publisher of advertising artwork from television commercials in the country. We created the first ever animation art lines for Coca-Cola, Anheuser-Bush, M&M/Mars, Pillsbury, Campbell Soup, Hershey's, etc. It was all pretty amazing. And all from that one ah-ha! moment standing in front of an old time Coca-Cola display.

I loved the animation business I was involved with and it did very well, but at a certain point I realized that at the end of the day, I didn't create the Coke Bears or the Bud Frogs for instance, and was always working with other's people's creations. I think it's common that many entrepreneurs want to create their own brand, their own characters and that's the creative force that drives so many of us.

So it was a little scary, but I made a conscious decision to completely reinvent my business. Suddenly instead of creating our animation artwork I was going to focus on a whole other business

15

and now we're going to just be making celebrity rubber ducks! But I always intuited from day one that the concept was unique enough and given time would definitely find it's market…and it did!

A common question I always get is: "You just make ducks?…you can make a living doing this?"…well, yeah!…if you make some of the finest ducks in the world and are the only ones in your niche producing them for celebrities, collegiate mascots, Fortune 500 companies, etc., you can easily become a millionaire doing it. Once you recognize that you have the means to create your own destiny, then everything becomes an opportunity, not an obstacle. So rather than wasting time thinking about what I could have or should have done, I found a way to create something different or better!

In my case, failure has created all my successes. When I didn't land the rights to market the Simpson's artwork, I detoured into commercial animation art which no one was doing. When one of the first factories we were working with began to act unethically and they, with a shady client, took us for over $15,000, it led to us finding a new factory with some of the best people possible whom we work with to this day. It never would have happened without that misfortune. Misfortune creates opportunities.

I personally never took a business course in my life. But when you feel a passion for doing something, trust me, I find that you will draw in the people around you to provide the expertise for areas you are weak in. Bottom line, your passion and energy will drive the business more than having a traditional business background.

I always say that people should read the stories of the people who created such amazing brands like Milton Hershey, Ben & Jerry, etc…it was their vision that made it all work. For me personally, these are the only kinds of business books I read – stories…stories about people…their hopes and dreams and how they made them a reality against all odds. Read enough books like that and you'll feel you can do anything.

I always tell every budding entrepreneur I meet that they should always know that you are never without options. Or to put it another way…so goes your mind goes the reality in front of you. I'm not talking psycho-babble mumbo jumbo. It's just the way the universe is structured and its workings are as tangible as touching a table. It's easy to think that when things aren't working out the way you hoped that you can feel trapped. Believe in that and that's pretty much the way things will unfold.

But if you can see every misfortune or difficult moment as nothing more than another moment ripe with potential and realize that you always have something you can do…then the energy gets freed up…things happen, orders arrive, people call, etc…so it really is best to never let your mind go into a space where you feel trapped. I don't know why they don't teach that in business school because to me it is at the heart of every successful business venture that had to overcome adversity. Anyway, that's pretty much it…again, sorry if it was too long, but hopefully there is something in there…

Also, if you want to see the final chapter in this story and the real ordeal of getting back up, please visit my website and click on the Made in America section on top. I just brought the whole rubber duck industry back to America where it was invented and am now the only one making rubber ducks in America once again! It was the hardest thing I have ever taken on and I can really share a lot of the ups and downs of that process.

# A Mission Trip; A Business Born From Sickness

*The Melanie Angelis Turnaround Story*

The Grecian Garden

www.thegreciangarden.com

Growing up, I loved nothing more than to drag a chair in front of the stove and cook with my grandma. Two entirely different cultures were at war in our household. We had my mom's southern roots and my dad's Greek roots shaping our every move including the food choices we made. I not only learned the secret to making my grandmother's famous McCormick mashed potatoes, but I also learned the secret to making the most succulent lamb you've ever tasted.

When I started college, stomachaches and overwhelming fatigue plagued me for a year before I started connecting the dots. I wanted a quick fix for my odd health problems, but doctors told me I needed more fiber or had the stomach flu. I ended up at the emergency room for chest pain, and still wasn't getting any answers. I finally turned to a naturopathic doctor, who asked if I'd ever traveled out of the country and possibly contracted anything.

Years prior, I traveled to Ecuador on a missions trip—in that moment, feelings of bitterness and resentment overwhelmed me. I realized there wouldn't be a quick fix for my health, regardless of what specialist I saw. It just wasn't fair. I shared Jesus with Ecuadorian villagers and here they had shared parasites with me.

After a few moments, I managed to look at the positive side. At least I now had some direction. I knew what was wrong with me and, armed with my bottles of herbal powders and potions, there was a ray of hope that healing was nearer. I started doing my own research and learned how to work with my body to heal my intestines. That was seven years ago, and today I can eat gluten and dairy and sugar—but I still don't, and I teach others how to live an allergy free life too. Eating whole foods and avoiding processed ones is the best way to heal the gut. In fact, the book I'm writing is called *The Grecian Garden: Where Diets, Calories, and Food Allergies Don't Exist.*

My passion to see others get well led me to starting my own business. I think some people are frightened by the concept because of the very real risk of failure. I started slowly and branched out as I discovered the needs my clients had. Instead of taking out loans or going into debt, I only invested what I could afford into my business. That way, I am free to focus on the aspects of my business that help the most people and bring me the most joy instead of just the most profitable ones. As I gained more education and clinical experience, I slowly transitioned my business to client consults and classes instead of catering healthy meals and desserts.

Both my healing and my business were a gradual process. Adding to the challenge, I moved from Florida to Ohio and back to Florida as my husband finished anesthesia school. He learned how to build me a website and figured out the licensing and tax forms we needed. Partnering with similar businesses was also a complex process so I could expand and network with like-minded individuals. I often tell new entrepreneurs to treat potential competitors well, because customers are better served by businesses that maintain their niche while working to collaborate with other businesses.

# How A Dog's Damage Helped Gary Start A Business

*The Gary Castelle Turnaround Story*

Sill Shield

www.SillShield.com

www.Personal-Reflectors.com

In 2005, I got a dog from the local shelter who loved to bark out the window. I didn't care but the windowsill took such a beating, a carpenter told me it would be easier (only $80) to "chisel it out & replace it" than to repair it. I looked everywhere for something to protect my new sill and found nothing. I was working for a plastics company at the time and one day the owner was commenting on falling sales (mostly due to the influx of cheap imports).

I was the newest employee at my level (five years) and I knew if there were going to be cut backs, I was the first to go. He said that he wished someone would come in with a brand new product line, unlike anything else, that they could produce. I told him that I wanted to create a windowsill protector and that if he would give me a good price on using his equipment to let me experiment, I'm sure I would come up with something. A month later, I had the first two sizes of the SILL SHIELD in my hand. A few months later, I volunteered to leave my job (the owner thanked me saying he just couldn't bring himself to lay me off). That night, I went to a jiffy online incorporation website and Magnum Plastics Inc of Greenwood Lake was founded (I was watching a rerun of an old

Magnum PI at the time).

My product line now consists of a wide selection of windowsill & door protectors as well as my new one-of-a-kind Velcro leash reflectors. Sales have increased every single year and I've never enjoyed my work so much. All my products are of my own design and made in the USA.

All of my products have my exclusive lifetime guarantee (as long as I'm alive, they're guaranteed – when I'm gone you're on your own) and my old company still produces nine sizes of Sill Shield.

I'm most proud of my latest creation, a unique Velcro reflector. It came to my attention that the #1 cause of death for children ages 4-15 is being struck by a vehicle.

One evening, I was behind a school bus and I noticed it was pinstriped with reflective tape. I thought it would be a better idea to make the kids reflective (I'm not really worried about hitting a bus). After some experimenting, I came up with the idea of mounting the reflective material on Velcro. Just peel one open & wrap it around any strap such as a dog leash, backpack, purse etc.

They are 2-sided to catch light from multiple directions, flexible, shatterproof, weatherproof, long lasting, easy to use, transferable and made in the USA.

# Pushed By Disability To Start My Own Business

*The Robert D Turnaround Story*

Sollars Security Shield

http://www.sollarssecurityshield.com/

I went blind in July 2003. The 17th to be exact. I woke up one morning and couldn't see clearly. It had happened before, but I didn't think anything of it. I figured it would clear up after my shower and getting to the office. It didn't.

I got to the office and while I was able to turn on the computer, I couldn't see the screen. So I wasn't able to start my job as the lead service coordinator for a temporary labor staffing company. I called my wife to come and pick me up.

I sat and wallowed in the idea that I couldn't work and I had people waiting to go out and go to work! She came and picked me up a few minutes later and the odyssey began. My wonderful wife, Eileen, immediately took me to the doctor and got me in to see an ophthalmologist that morning. I was soon diagnosed with detached retinas. The result was severely hampered eyesight.

The retinal surgeon told us that he had never seen anyone with such prolific retinopathy that could still see out of his good eye! Dr. Gordon said that the extra blood vessels were floating around in my eye like seaweed in the ocean! And because they were so prolific, they pulled the retina from the back of the eye. And it was all due to my uncontrolled diabetes. I soon found out that

23

both eyes were the same, but the left was worse.

Starting at the end of July (the best 42nd birthday gift – yes it was my birthday!), I had the first of four surgeries, two in each eye. None of them worked. I am now totally blind.

To say the transition was difficult is to say that Mt. Everest is a small hill. It was a long road to go and I almost lost Eileen because of my not understanding where the words, anger, and depression were coming from. Finally, it took another severe blow to bring me under control. I found out in 2011 that my kidneys were failing and I would need a transplant. Therefore my blood sugars are under control, my weight is down and I'm doing okay.

However, the one issue I had throughout this entire time was that I couldn't go back to work. I was a person who thrived on constantly having something to do and moving about. I couldn't work in a normal office environment and trying to listen to my computer and someone talking in the other ear, as a customer service rep wasn't in the cards either.

So I decided to start my own business doing what I love and know I can do. And while it is a bit unusual for someone who is blind to be in my field, I have more than thirty years of experience in it (I kept up when I wasn't working). That field you ask? Security.

I couldn't find anyone to hire me for a job in security during the height of the 'recession' doing what I do, which is training and consulting in workplace/school violence prevention and security officer operations. Every time I would talk to someone they stared at me like I was stupid. So when I was at a networking event my wife perfected the 'adoring wife look' so they would know to address me and not her. This is not an easy stereotype to overcome.

I would go out on sales calls and the person who made the appointment was 'hot' to get me into the office to talk about what I do, but once they saw me I got the 'bums rush' out the door. For someone who was really concerned about workplace violence, they barely gave me 5 minutes of time to discuss it! I don't do well in crowds and never have, so Eileen helped me immensely with those things. The biggest obstacle I have at this point is finding the sales leads and making those cold calls. Eileen has a full-time job and can't help me as much as I need her to, so I am trying to find my way in this. Publicity is one way to do that. I write, and go on the radio and talk. I've given a couple of seminars and have been well received.

But there is still the blindness obstacle to overcome and that is the hardest part. I do have a book that I will be self-publishing this fall as an e-book and hope that brings me some recognition. I want to help save lives of adults and kids and at this point it gets frustrating when I can't do that using my own natural talents.

I am certainly hoping for a positive outcome soon. I want to be off of government disability and take care of my wife again, the way I used to and the way it should be. I don't like her having to support the family and my medical bills and me contributing nothing except a few bucks a month. It is, as the saying goes in Missouri, 'A hard row to hoe!' not to mention frustrating! But the only thing I can do is what I have done my entire life. Keep pushin' on 'til the end.

# A Girl's Dream Birthday Gift; The American Dream!

*The Vienne Cheung Turnaround Story*

VienneMilano

www.VienneMilano.com

So, a little about myself. I was born in Hong Kong and moved to Brookline, Mass at the age of six. From an early age, I had a love of fashion and the move was especially exciting for me when I recognized the drastic difference in styles. In fact, it became a dream of mine to start a fashion brand derived from my experience. Around age 11, I remember forerunning flare sleeved shirts (which I ripped off from Seventeen magazine) and met some ridicule from my classmates. Yet, it didn't stop me dreaming. Along the same line, I had a list of things that I had wanted to achieve – my bucket list. And one of the things on the list was to start a fashion business.

Ever since I was a girl, I knew that I wanted to make an impact in the world. I always knew that I wanted to do something different from everyone else.

I believe that accessories allow a woman to make a statement for herself, particularly hosiery. And as a teenager, I purchased stockings from Asia as they were very different from the ones I found in the US. Later, I traveled to Italy with a high school choir where I was surrounded by beautiful things and I discovered Italian hosiery.

Fast forward twenty years and I worked in the Products department of a high tech company in Cambridge, Mass. I was involved with the launch process of multimillion dollar software products that would make the internet "go faster". Although I enjoyed where I was at, I didn't find what I was doing to be particularly fulfilling. I asked myself: if I looked back twenty-five years from now, would I be content with what I have accomplished or would I be happier knowing that I challenged myself in doing something even greater?

I had arrived at a point when I questioned my ambition and revisited my childhood dream.

On several occasions ranging from Valentine's Day dinner to everyday office wear, I wasn't able to find suitable thigh highs. Everything I found was associated with Halloween costumes or lacked the essential feature of a silicone band. It occurred to me that there was a gap in the US hosiery market. Serendipitously, I met an Italian investor who was involved with a trading company and was opened to the idea to creating a luxury hosiery brand. After many years of wanting to start a business, I was suddenly given the opportunity to do what I have always dreamed of: to launch a fashion business.

I must admit, I was intimidated by the idea. Do I *really* want to give up my lucrative salary? Are a secure job and a stress-free life worth not trying to make an impact in the world? And what if my business does not succeed? But then I remember all of the amazing people who succeeded, as they had nothing to lose. I am not married, and I don't have kids. This is the time of my life where I can afford to make mistakes without jeopardizing the lives of others. If I had a family, I would not want to be in a position that would put them in financial risk (of course there are countless very successful "mompreneurs" – whose work cannot be undermined). However, why put myself in that situation when I don't have to? Timing was sudden, and the decision was not easy. I finally decided to leave corporate America as a present to myself a – 30th birthday present no less.

Over the course of 9 months, I worked relentlessly with my investor creating a collection of elegant thigh highs that would be appropriate for the American market. Although both of us had dabbled in the world of fashion, neither of us had a solid background in the industry. As such, the traditional methods of launching a brand were restricted. So we first began with a marketing lesson. I researched the market and it was clear to me that 1) hosiery is making a comeback in America and 2) other women have also been looking for elegant thigh high stockings.

With that in mind, it led to our brand positioning: *VienneMilano is the first luxury hosiery dedicated exclusively to thigh high stockings. Our products are Made In Italy for women who want to reveal their style and confidence by being elegant, playful, and sexy in every occasion.* To clarify, we believe that in order for a woman to reveal something, she has to have something to show. As such, we target women who have style and confidence to reveal. We also aimed at playing up the fact that thigh highs is an elegant wear and play down on its sexy attributes. And lastly, we want to introduce thigh highs as an accessory that can be worn for every occasion. We wanted to inspire women that by wearing VienneMilano, it gives her an extra boast of confidence.

A long time ago, miniskirts and bikinis were donned as something that was considered crazy. Today, it is perceived as something that's essential in every woman's wardrobe. This is where I want thigh highs to be.

*"In prosperity our friends know us; in adversity we know our friends."* - John Churton Collins. No matter how proud and or happy your friends are of your work – let's face it, you will be alone. Although I had a brilliant investor and business partner, this was my venture and the daily decisions were mine to make. Unless they are also entrepreneurs (which is even harder to get their time), your friends and family are not always going to understand why you gave up your 9-5 jobs to work 24/7.

They are also not going to understand why you don't hang out as often or why you geek out at every learning opportunity. And they are not always going to be happy or excited for you over small wins. Not even your mother may understand why you began your business. However, that's okay because those who are closest to you will understand that regardless of your business, you are doing something that fulfills you. Your true friends will vouch for you without having their ego and or self-centeredness get in the way and those are the friends you keep for life. And although it's sad that there aren't many people like this left in the world, that's OK. You want to be with those who matter.

Today, I have learned a lot from my first year of business. The story is certainly not over. Although I am happy with what we've accomplished, we have a long way to go. I am grateful for the friends and family who supported the building of the brand.

# The Light bulb Moment That Lit A Path To The Oprah Show

*The Lori Cheek Turnaround Story*

Cheeked.com

www.cheekd.com

I'm Lori Cheek, an architect turned entrepreneur, Founder and CEO of Cheekd.com– the reverse engineered dating site. After working in architecture, furniture and design for fifteen years for companies such as Christian Dior, Vitra & Karkula, I came up with an idea that led me into the NYC World of Tech and am now solving missed connections one card at a time. I'm no longer building structures, I'm now building relationships and it's a lot more fun.

Nearly five years ago, I was out to dinner with a friend & architectural colleague and I had excused myself from the table. When I returned, my handsome dinner date had scribbled on the back of his business card, "want to have dinner?" As we were leaving the restaurant, he slid that card to an attractive woman at a nearby table.

{{{{{LIGHTBULB}}}}} It had happened to me a thousand times during my NYC commute—spotting that intriguing stranger on a train, in a café, crossing the street, at baggage claim, etc. and nearly 999 of them got away. Handing a business card could have been one answer, but I was entranced by the mysterious gesture of handing it to the object of your affection and removing the personal details included on a typical business card, which is simply too much information to hand to a total stranger. A person's name on a card, alone, could potentially lead you to their front door.

My solution to the problem would apply a personal approach to online dating by moving the initial encounter offline with a smooth physical introduction. In May of 2010, I launched Cheekd.com—my solution to the 999 missed opportunities I'd personally experienced. Shortly after launch, the New York Times proclaimed, "Move over, Match.com" and coined Cheek'd as "the next generation of online dating." A few days after that article, I saw this email pop up in my inbox:

"Hello, I am a producer at The Oprah Winfrey Show. I am looking to talk to Lori Cheek about Cheekd.com. I can be reached at 312.633.****. Thank you and I look forward to hearing from you soon."

They asked for a deck of cards and a photo of me followed by a short phone interview. I cried for nearly an hour. I called my parents to tell them and they couldn't even understand what I was trying to say, then my mom couldn't stop crying which made me start crying all over again. I couldn't believe my "little" dating card idea had lead to a call from Oprah. My life has pretty much been turned inside out (in the most amazing way) from that day forward.

Building Cheek'd has been an incredible learning experience. I've taken a major risk (both financially & mentally), but my heart and mind are in this project every waking moment. I've never been more dedicated to anything. Despite the occasional overwhelming stress, it's been loads of fun. I spend a lot of my time guerilla marketing and slipping Cheek'd Cards into pockets, hoods, bags, etc. My favorite story to date would be the personal Lori Cheek'ng of Hip Hop Mogul, Russell Simmons: http://www.observer.com/2010/style/russell-simmons-gets-cheekd-chanel-soho-opening.

In the process, I couldn't even begin to count the number of times I've failed building my business over the past few years. I've learned to welcome the mistakes and even joke that I've learned so much from them that I'm going to keep making more of them on purpose. I've taken a crash course in building a business and failing has probably been the greatest lesson of all. Making mistakes at least means you're trying.

I've bootstrapped this business for the past two-and-a-half years. I used my savings from my fifteenth year career in architecture (til it ran out), then started selling my designer clothes (used to work as an architect at Dior) at consignment shops and on ebay, rented out my apartment on AirBnB for fourteen months ('til I nearly got evicted) and am now doing focus groups and selling my electronics and other odds and ends around my apartment on Craigslist. I've done everything I know how to do and ultimately, I've built a brand and a company and thousands of people are using the service all over the world. It's the most rewarding feeling.

After decades on my own relentless pursuit for love, one day last summer, I was sitting solo at a Crab Shack in Montauk and with no AT&T signal, I decided to toss my best friend, "iPhone," into my beach bag. When I looked up, a mysterious, gorgeous man in Ray Bans and a baseball cap sitting right next to me said, "Nice tattoos." I handed him the Cheek'd card that reads, "let's meet for a drink." We met for that drink and we're engaged to get married this year.

# A Pit–Bull's Image That Led To A Picture–Perfect Business

*The Sarah Gross Turnaround Story*

Rescue Chocolate

RescueChocolate.com

It all started with a thumbnail image of a forlorn pit-bull. Her name was Mocha, and her photo had been posted online by her foster mom as a desperate act to find her a permanent home before the clock ran down to zero.

Mocha's eyes stuck with me. I flashed through that online posting once, twice, and then again. I kept going back to check on her, to see if by some miracle an angel had descended and adopted her. I had grown up sharing my house with dogs and volunteering at my local animal shelter, but I knew I couldn't have a dog at the moment–I was never home, and I lived in the middle of the biggest concrete jungle in the world, New York City. Besides, the building in which I rented a room didn't even allow pets.

Those beautiful mocha-brown eyes.... It took awhile to track down the email address of her foster mom. I set up an appointment just to meet Mocha on the Upper East Side of Manhattan, with no strings attached. Dear Reader, you absolutely know what happened next.

Mocha leapt into my arms. A bit later, we rode in a taxi together back to Brooklyn. My four housemates and the landlord were informed of the new regime, and I started searching for my new apartment, near the park. Mocha put on much-needed weight and her coat turned silky. And then, a few months later, she handed me a wallop of inspiration.

I was savoring the last bite of a dark chocolate bar before heading out for our morning walk (doesn't everyone eat chocolate for breakfast?!). The empty wrapper from that bar joined hundreds of others in a chocolate album that I had been keeping, as a hobby. (I'm a vegan, and I enjoy finding and sampling luscious, cruelty-free foods.) Powered up by the chipotle-chili-chocolate bar, I hit the sidewalk with my gorgeous best friend.

Suddenly it occurred to me: why not put together my two loves? How about developing a scrumptious new dark chocolate bar, selling it, and donating the profits to animals in need?

I already worked part-time at a raw vegan chocolate factory in Queens, where I had developed a best-selling flavor. I had a few contacts in the chocolate industry. I knew what tasted good. And God knew there was certainly a need to raise awareness about the epidemic of pet overpopulation in America. The idea for Rescue Chocolate was almost fully formed before Mocha and I returned from our walk that morning in December 2009.

Now, working with executive chef Jean Francois Bonnet at the Tumbador chocolate factory, I am having a blast dreaming up new flavors for my line of dark chocolate products, naming them, selling them, and choosing the animal rescue charities to support each month. Rescue Chocolate is carried by a number of retail outlets in New York, Boston, Chicago, and elsewhere, and it is also sold online.

People give it a try and become addicted. Maybe it has something to do with the picture of the pooch on the wrapper of every Rescue Chocolate bar—that one with the mocha-brown eyes.

# A Little Pressure Goes A Long Way

*The Chris Kimball Turnaround Story*

CK Financial Services

http://moneyconcepts.com/ckimball

This year I will celebrate twenty years as a financial planner. During that time I've achieved many milestones, industry designations, advanced degrees, and accolades. Looking at the plaques on my wall, one would think I was the epitome of the successful, self-confident entrepreneur.

Well, success is a relative term, so that might be a bit hard to quantify. I'm definitely an entrepreneur; I own my office condo and have 5 staff on the payroll. When it comes to self-confidence, though, I don't think I'll ever reach my desired comfort zone.

My business has certainly grown and become more secure, but it's still pretty much an "eat-what-you-kill" profession. Perhaps a healthy dose of worry is what keeps me motivated; I know that's exactly what caused me to work as hard as I did at the beginning of this career.

I was born a musician; at 4 years old I was playing drums on a small drum set my dad made for me out of Folgers' coffee cans and 2X4s. As I grew, I played in school and college bands, as well as local Rock and Roll groups. The Rock and Roll made me some money, but even after touring nationally with a couple of bands, I realized I needed a real job.

I began in electronics sales, went back to the University of Washington for a B.A. in advertising, worked for a year in that field, hated it and went back to electronics sales. Electronics, however, was a rapidly changing business, and as the products got less expensive, the commissions got crushed.

I was again forced to make the decision as to what I wanted to be when I grew up.

In 1993 my wife's aunt, Barbara Burgess, suggested I consider a career in the financial services industry. She had worked at a major insurance company for most of her career, and felt it might be a good fit for me.

At first I was hesitant. "I don't want to sell insurance," I protested. She assured me there was much more to it than that, and I should at least explore the possibility. She said I'd be able to work with individuals, families and business owners helping them to plan their financial future and reach their goals. That didn't sound too bad, so I thought I'd look into it.

I was interviewed by the local manager of the insurance company for which Barbara worked, followed by an interview with the Regional Director. I took a number of tests and must have achieved adequate grades, because shortly thereafter I was notified I had the job.

At first, I was relieved. It soon dawned on me, however, that I was embarking on a career in which I had almost no experience. Not only that, although there was a small draw account from which I would receive a minimal salary, I was responsible for selling enough to keep the account filled. If I didn't do as well as I needed to, the account would soon be empty, as would my wallet!

My wife, Vicki, and I had recently welcomed our second son into the world and because of our expanding family, we had decided to purchase a larger home. Vicki decided to reduce her hours as a

CPA to half-time so she could be at home with our sons. What this meant was that within a few months, our expenses increased, our income was reduced and our mortgage tripled.

Nothing like a little pressure to produce!

I remember my first six months at the new job. I had to drive from Tacoma to Seattle every Monday morning during rush-hour for a 30-minute meeting, only to then turn around and drive back to Tacoma. I was responsible for calling prospects, making appointments, filling out paperwork and following through with any policy or account I initiated. It was a lot of work, and a lot of stress.

Some days as I drove to my office in downtown Tacoma I would become so nervous I would experience dry heaves—sometimes so severe I'd have to pull to the side of the road to compose myself. When I arrived at the office I would hold my breath as I approached my inbox, fearful I'd see a cluster of pink slips indicating some (or all!) of my appointments for the day had canceled. When that happened, a sick feeling would come over me as I realized that week would net me almost no paycheck.

There's an interesting thing about stress and pressure; although they cause great discomfort, they also are very effective motivators. My first year in the business, I sold more policies than anyone else in the entire Pacific Northwest agency. I was even awarded a new laptop computer for my efforts. That helped build my confidence enough to keep me in a business which typically averages only thirteen percent retention over four years.

Even though I had a contract that allowed me to market and sell products and services from outside the main insurance company for which I worked, and even though I was my own boss, I was still considered a statutory employee and therefore under my main company's compliance regulations. Over the years the rules became more onerous and unmanageable, so two years ago I left my original company and went completely independent.

Going independent was a significant change, but looking back over the successes of the prior eighteen years gave me the confidence I needed to take that leap of faith. It turns out to have been a good decision and things are going well.

Starting my business twenty years ago was terrifying. The good news is, however, now that I've been doing this so long, I'm only scared *some* of the time!

# Driven By A Passion; Start Of A Business That Matters!

*The Thomas Boley Turnaround Story*

Hawkins, Boley & AlDabbagh

www.bandalawfirm.com/

I moved from my home state of Iowa to practice law in Las Vegas in 2008. When I moved here, I dreamed of the glamorous life and living in the glow of the neon lights of the Las Vegas Strip. I took the bar exam, passed, and took a job with a large firm. The lifestyle at a large firm in Vegas ·is as horrid as people describe in bigger cities. I had always dreamed of starting a law firm, but I thought I needed some grey hairs before anyone would take me seriously.

I left the big firm and started practicing personal injury law for a small firm. After some disagreements with the partners, I left that firm and found myself in the worst job market in history for attorneys. After searching for a new job, my fiancé and I determined that I should start a solo practice.

In July 2010, I signed a lease for an office and put out my shingle. It was slow going, and I didn't make very much money, but I survived thanks to some great mentors. I also discovered my passion for criminal defense during that period. The life was hard for a year, and I ended up moonlighting at a Las Vegas nightclub for a time.

In January 2011, my fiancé left because of the crazy lifestyle my business had created. Unfortunately, she could not see the light at the end of the tunnel. This sent me to a dark place for a while. I learned about my own thresholds and came face to face with my inner demons. A few months later, I was able to stop moonlighting and I met my first business partner. I merged with another young lawyer and we saw a great deal of success in a very short time.

I pulled myself together, and now we have a very successful business. We later acquired the solo practice of a bankruptcy attorney. We are now a three-partner firm in Las Vegas practicing in personal injury, criminal defense, and bankruptcy law. I love my life, even though I had to sacrifice to get here.

# The Journey From Fears To: World Tours, First-Class Travel and President Obama

*The Dan Nainan Turnaround Story*

Dan Nainan

www.nainan.com

A little background – I was a senior engineer with Intel Corporation. My job was to travel the world with Chairman Andy Grove, doing technical demonstrations on stage at events, and I was incredibly nervous about speaking on stage. I took a comedy class to get over the fear, and the comedy kind of took off.

Since then, I have performed at the Democratic National Convention, at a TED Conference, at three presidential inaugural events, for Hillary Clinton, for Donald Trump at his golf course in Palm Beach, for Apple cofounder Steve Wozniak and for many similar luminaries. I recently performed at the Kennedy Center in Washington DC and on the MDA Labor Day Telethon with Carrot Top and Penn and Teller. Also, I appeared in an Apple Get a Mac commercial. I perform all over the States as well as in many foreign countries. My life is like that of George Clooney in Up in the Air, just without the sex LOL.

Click here <https://vimeo.com/63621461> to see President Barack Obama call me Hilarious, & testimonials from Hillary Clinton, Mayors Michael Bloomberg & Antonio Villaraigosa, CNN's Dr. Sanjay Gupta, Editor Arianna Huffington, tech luminaries Steve

Wozniak, Vinod Khosla, Steve Case, Andy Grove & Leo Laporte, Ford CEO Bill Ford, Comedians Russell Peters & Robert Schimmel, US Senators Al Franken & Bob Casey, Actors Kunal Nayyar, Ashley Judd, Connie Sellecca, John Tesh, Aasif Mandvi, John Hodgman, Justin Long, Tim Conway & Leonardo Nam, Motivational Humorist Judy Carter, President Obama's Sister Maya Soetoro-Ng, US Attorneys Preet Bharara & Kamala Harris

# While Stuck In An Elevator, A New Business Comes Up!

*The Ellen Weiss Turnaround Story*

The Impact Elevator

www.theimpactelevator.com

I worked at ad agencies for years. As a senior account executive my job was to hunt down new business, pitch them the big idea, and then drag back profitable work for the agency. Many times I struggled because the clients I brought in were not always the most ethical people that one could meet. Still, work was work. Projects that I pitched and won meant a lot of people had jobs to show up for every day. It was early summer, 2010, and the economy was so very weak.

My boss sent me to make a pitch for a new piece of business with a pharmaceutical company in the area. A big part of the pitch was our agency's plan to raise "awareness" of the need for this drug by creating an insecurity where none likely existed. Great – my work would make prospective consumers feel worse about themselves so that they would demand a prescription for a potentially intrusive medication from their doctor to "fix" this newly discovered "defect."

I asked to be excused from the whole project. No go. On the appointed day I suited up, packed up my pitch and headed out. I parked my car about a block away and slowly made my way up the busy city street. Every step was a struggle. Everything about who I was and what I believed was going to have to be set aside to make this presentation.

It felt awful. I had twenty minutes to spare and stopped in a coffee shop for a jolt-inducing coffee. Made a pit stop in the restroom. Bought a big cookie and a bottle of water and stashed them in my purse – for later. "Enough with the delaying tactics," I told myself. "Just get on with it."

The security desk in the building handed me an access badge and I climbed aboard the elevator for the ride the to twelfth floor. I was alone in this cold, steely space and preparing to step off the elevator all smiles and confidence and strength. Between the fifth and sixth floors I heard a scratching, rumbling noise from above, and the elevator stopped. Jarringly, suddenly, and quite completely – stopped.

No buzzing, lights or announcements came forth as I hit the emergency button. Silence. I texted the prospective client, five and half floors above – they said they would call building security. I expected rescue in mere minutes. An hour later, the building super texted me that they were "working the problem." Twenty minutes later the client texted that they were rescheduling the meeting.

I slumped to the floor, relieved. And then I laughed out loud. Sometimes God taps you on the shoulder and suggests a better way around a problem. This time God smacked me with a bat. I sat on the floor and opened up my laptop. I drafted a short and polite letter of resignation from the agency, effective immediately. Over the next two hours, I typed up a business plan for my own agency, crafted a mission statement, and happily tapped out the name of my new branding and advertising agency: The Impact Elevator.

My work centers on non-profits and solo and small practice professional service practices.

46

# A Business Built Through Chaos

*The Holly Jo Anderson Turnaround Story*

Veritas Marketing

www.veritasmarketing.com

I started my business in May of 2001, with two partners, after our then boss asked me to sell an ESOP (Employee Stock Ownership Plan) to the employees. Before I agreed to do that, I did a little homework on ESOPs. It turns out that his company wasn't large enough to qualify to be an ESOP. That explained why he was buying failing small advertising agencies and design firms.

So essentially, he was asking me to sell a certificate of debt to my co-workers and asking that I also take on this newly acquired debt. As retirement plans go, I'm sure that would have been very nice for him. However, I respectfully declined to take on that roll. He said, "It's my way or the highway." I said, "Okay." What he didn't do the math on was the amount of his total sales that were coming from me.

He also likely didn't remember that I did not have a non-compete agreement.

I come from a long line of entrepreneurs. My grandfather had a cement contracting business. Both of my parents started and owned various businesses and at the time that I started my business, two of my five siblings had businesses. That number is now five out of five. Growing up with two parents running small businesses proved to me that I didn't want to do it. Never say never.

Within every company I ever worked for, I was a bit of an odd duck. My specialty was and still is, industrial-based marketing. I like to market things that you would never expect. Typically, my customer's target audience is engineers or architects. Our clients do everything from manufacture component parts for semi-truck engines to manufacture and market acoustical testing chambers and underground ductwork. All I really ever needed was an art department. And I sort of ran this goofy little business from the back of wherever I was working. My last employer was the closest fit for my calling. They provided business-to-business marketing and advertising services. He hired me as his Director of Client Services.

My specialty always made it somewhat of a challenge to find a job. Every time I hit the job application trail, I received advice from multiple advertising agency owners to start my own business. My last job transition wasn't any different. This time, I actually listened. I asked myself, "Why don't you start your own?" The answer was that I didn't know what I didn't know about starting a business. In other words, the fear of what I didn't know was holding me back.

So I typed in starting a business in Minnesota into Google. Up popped a seminar put on by SCORE Minneapolis called "Going into Business." On a side note, a few years after I started my own business, I became the marketing presenter for the Going Into Business seminars put on by the SCORE☐organization. I signed up and attended the all-day event. I called my then soon-to-be partners during the lunch break and said, "We can so do this."

I spent the next two nights writing our business plan. I signed up for a mentor through the SCORE organization. A week after the seminar, I received a call on my office phone from the mentor they aligned us with. He could not have been a better fit for us. He actually started a business-to-business agency that is now pretty large and switched its focus to business-to-consumer. He even managed one of my clients when he owned his agency.

One of my then partners and I met with the mentor to review the business plan. He didn't see why it wouldn't work and gave us some sage advice – buy matching furniture.

I was still employed at the time and had no intention of quitting until I had an office rented, etc. My boss actually hired a private investigator to follow me around. This unmarked white van would show up everywhere. And the driver wasn't all that discrete about taking photos of me. The day my car went into the shop and I got a rental – I was bombarded when I got back to the office by the upper management asking me what happened to my car.

Clearly, the PI couldn't find me or track me that day. I just smiled. My former boss took it to the level of having the IT department hack into my personal computer while he had me called into an office for a meeting. All of this was later confirmed in the deposition for the lawsuit he filed on us for breach of the loyalty law. I, however, was smart enough to hire an attorney and discuss it with him prior to even seeing the mentor. I already knew about the loyalty law and what my obligations were. And I most certainly did not break the loyalty law.

This all became too much to deal with while trying to start a business. So, I wrote letters to my clients and a resignation letter about one month before I had planned. I walked in and grabbed my coffee cup; everything else was already out of the office. I tossed my resignation letter on his desk with a simple good-bye. I did a little hoop in the parking lot. I stopped at the mailbox on my way out of the area and mailed all the letters. I called every client as soon as I had gotten home. And a business was born.

I worked from my home for about one-and-a-half months with one of my partners until we had the office all set up. Then our third partner joined us. We were in the black in the second month.

The nasty legal letters started showing up at my house on day two. I had to have the Geek-Squad wipe my computer hard drive clean because he said that I had proprietary information on my personal laptop, which I didn't. But I complied anyway.

It took about three months before the actual lawsuit was filed. We had to collect anything we had from the company, which ended up amounting to check stubs and commission reports that came with my checks. The deposition was on 9-11. I refused to leave even though the buildings downtown were being closed.

Luckily, the attorneys and court reporter also remained for the entire six-hour deposition. Twenty-five thousand dollars in legal fees later, it was tossed out of federal court.

Shortly after the lawsuit was dismissed, my office fell victim to arson. Someone literally kicked a hole in my window over my desk, dumped in gasoline, tossed in the entire container for good measure and struck a match. They were never able to prove who the arsonist was. Electronics and sprinklers don't mix. Thankfully, I was a stickler for backups. I borrowed one of my friend's small son's computer to keep it going. We were also asked to leave the building and find a new office shortly after the incident.

My business partners left about five years in. One of them inherited some money and the other one wasn't cut out for business ownership. And we're still moving forward today.

# The Late Bloomer - Business Start Up At 65!

*The Anthony P. Nestora Turnaround Story*

Back Up Better

www.backupbetter.com

I am now age 66 going on 67 in October of 2013. was a financial planner for forty years. It was the only job I ever had and I always worked for somebody as a commission salesman, didn't ever own the business. That's all changed now. When I was 65, after forty years, I was burnt out, couldn't do the financial planning anymore for a lot of reasons. It wasn't fun anymore, I had less patience, and the markets were bad. All in all, I just wanted out but I hadn't saved enough money to completely retire, far from it.

So I needed something to do and I needed to generate income for living expenses as well. I decided to go with the flow and do something automotive as I have always been a car nut, and I felt selling and marketing on-line was the way to go. I lived quite a lavish lifestyle, raced Porsches for ten years, big house, etc. Now all that was coming back to haunt me and I needed to do something quick, but most importantly, something I would like to do on an ongoing basis.

I had learned about an automotive product, a rear window fresnel lens for SUV's, minivans, and station wagons that DOUBLES your vision into that Blind Zone right behind these vehicles. That blind zone ranges from 14-50 feet depending on the individual vehicle. Now here is the opportunity and it's paying off nicely so far. Scary but true, over fifty times EVERY WEEK a parent or relative backs over a young child in a driveway or parking lot, often fatally.

Between 200 and 300 children are killed in back over accidents every year and thousands are injured seriously. And, thousands of non-fatal incidents go unreported each year as well. So the opportunity was with Soccer Moms, who drive these types of vehicles and are rushing around and on the go all day long chauffeuring their kids around to all the activities today's kids have. When you rush, accidents will happen and children are unpredictable. In any event again, these back over accidents occur more than fifty times every week, often fatally!

New and/or newer cars now come with backup cameras. There has so far, according to KidsAndCars.org, not been one fatal accident with a vehicle that has a backup camera. So who is causing all these back over accidents? The other eighty to ninety million SUV's, minivans, and station wagons sold over the last twenty years who are driving around with no additional vision aids and thus, limited rearward and outward vision.

That's my market, the pre-backup camera vehicles already on the road and driving around with severely limited rearward vision. My Fresnel Lens is 8×10 and made of optical grade PVC flexible plastic, only 1/16th of an inch thick. It is inexpensive, very easy to install or uninstall, very effective, and most importantly, it saves lives.

I own Back Up Better, LLC and we sell vehicle safety products. I work out of my house and use part of my garage as my shop. I sell most of my lenses and add-on blind spot mirrors thru Mommy Bloggers and there are a ton of them. For little or no fee, they will do a product review, tell my story, and often we do giveaways and contests to foster more interest. So far so good. We are on Facebook and Twitter, and have appeared in articles in magazines and local newspapers.

# A Tragedy That Led To Total Business Health

*The Michelle Hastie Turnaround Story*

Total Body Health Solutions

www.totalbodyhealthsolutions.com

It's funny how you didn't realize you were going to be an entrepreneur and then once you stumble into that role you wonder how you could possibly have done anything else. I certainly had no idea that running my own business was in my cards, yet here I am… four years later at the age of 26, running my own business.

I truly thought I would be a personal trainer at a corporate gym the rest of my life. Then I stepped into a management role and realized the company was, quite frankly, not run in a way I could stand. Which left me with a decision: work for another gym or start my own thing. With the nudging of my very supportive boyfriend, (who is now my fiancé); I began a brand new business as a personal trainer.

I don't know if you believe in signs or not, yet just 2 weeks after I started my new business, I received one that truly made me ask myself if I had made the right decision. I was in a tragic car accident that left me completely immobile. I was stuck on the couch, unable to work and not even able to move.

It seems appropriate to take a step back for second, though, and talk about something that is a huge epidemic in our society, excess weight. When I first started as a personal trainer, I walked around the gym in a thin, 120 lb frame, not much muscle mass but not stick skinny either. Yet I never really felt like I fit in. I was honestly not athletic at all and was given the position purely due to my outgoing likable personality and was taught to do everything else. I made a decision that I was going to do whatever it took to look like a personal trainer. Fast forward to the day of my car accident, I was miserable weighing 25 lbs more than my first day on the job and it wasn't muscle mass, it was all fat.

For the first time in my life, I was massively struggling with my weight. I tried everything including working out 2x day/7x a week, eating 1500 calories a day, you know "Biggest Loser" style! My weight simply wouldn't budge. On the day of my car accident, as I was hit by five different vehicles, then realizing I was lucky to be alive, I was left with yet another decision. If I couldn't lose weight working out all the time, what was going to happen to me as I lay on the couch unable to move? This was quickly replaced by the thought of, "Who the hell cares? You need to get back to your business which requires moving and this weight thing is out of your control right now."

So I chose to surrender to the weight thing and focus on getting healthy and moving to get back to my business. Funny thing happens when you surrender and relax… results happen. In just one month my body managed to shed 10 lbs while lying on the couch, not moving around. Absurd isn't it? Just the opposite of everything we are told. Here I was once again defying science. Although this time, I was happy to do it.

This began my curiosity, how does weight loss really work? I studied, I worked under various mentors, I got certified in everything that had anything to do with how our minds work with our bodies and I founded Total Body Health Solutions. It is a weight loss coaching business that allows people to lose weight by first healing the mental stuff going on in their lives creating weight gain and then living their life free of the excess weight forever.

I am happy to report I reached my goal weight very quickly and have kept that weight off to this day without any effort. I enjoy food, I eat what I want and I no longer overeat or binge eat. I work out when I want, I don't when I don't want to and my clothes always fit. And I now turn around and teach this to all the other dieters in the world so that they too can free themselves of the insanity of dieting, and truly live their lives in a body they love.

# The Act Of Balancing Entrepreneurship and Family Life

*The Christopher Robbins Turnaround Story*

Familius LLC

www.familius.com

After seventeen years running someone else's business, I resigned my position as CEO, threw caution to the wind, and launched my own book publishing company. Yes, it is crazy.

First, I'm no stranger to entrepreneurship. I sold more zucchini from our family garden by pulling my red wagon around our suburban Utah neighborhood than the local grocery store. My pitch was, "How do you know if you don't have any friends? You have to buy your own zucchini." Since you could get a baker's dozen from me, you weren't really buying them all and could count a young boy named Christopher Robbins as your friend. (Being named after a story book character had its advantages.)

I also launched two unsuccessful businesses in the nineties. My first book-publishing venture died when my partner died. It was a bad omen. My second venture was a brilliant digital-only publishing company in 1999 that provided fiction as serial email deliveries. We called it Novelocity and our tagline was Your Daily Serial. It died after I focused 100 percent of my energy on getting venture capital (it was the late nineties!) and after flying in Lear Jets to New York where young Internet firms offered to build our site for $5,000,000, on average, and offered us plates of exotic cheeses. We were dreaming of being millionaires.

In March of 2000 as my partner and I were sitting in the boardroom of our chief investor, picking up a check for the first major investment, our investor, the CEO of a large tech company, received a call from the largest shareholder of the company. The market crash of 2000 had started that day and our check came off the table, literally. We flew home watching the Dow Jones and NASDAQ plummet, wiping out fortunes. And we were left owning a company with no content and no money. Stupid.

Having been disappointed twice and having a young family, I focused full energy on building someone else's business that was months from bankruptcy. It had not paid its independent sales force in eighteen months and its printers for over a year. Its debt to equity was a staggering 48 to 1. The interest alone on the printer notes was 18 percent per month! We worked, strategized, worked, strategized, worked and got lucky every year through 2008, growing from 20 to 35 percent a year, paying off the loans, building backlist, adding infrastructure, building warehouses and office space, having best sellers, believing that we were smart . . . It was fantastic.

We had made serious money, growing from under two million to twenty-six million, by betting on the housing and textbook markets. Then the housing bubble of 2008 killed both markets and we shed half our revenue in months. I had left the company vulnerable and that decision was a job killer, a spirit killer, and a mission killer. While we preserved the company, our decisions took a tremendous toll and it was time for me to go.

Now that I've launched yet another company and have been working day-in and day-out for almost a year, what are the differences? Is one better than another? I've come to believe that everything has its opposite so I come to entrepreneurship believing that one isn't necessarily better than another. It's different and each has its pros and cons.

But I do have some observations:

Workload

I've never been a nine-to-five guy and I'm in startup mode. So, this point might not be fair. Further, my eyes are always bigger than my stomach and I'm creating a company from scratch that went from nothing to seventy contracted titles, twenty published titles, a full interactive crowdsourcing and social media-enriched website in six months. It's crazy. I spend on□average twelve to fourteen hours a day working on this new company. I hear about people spending eighteen hours a day on ventures, and I'm not sure how that's possible as you have to eat something, take a shower, use the rest room, sleep, get dressed, and if you are married, as I am, and have kids, as I do (9), there has to be time to, at the very least, talk to them or you can work your way out of the family pretty quick. And, forgive the preaching, but I believe that no success can compensate for failure in the home.

When I was running the other company, I often put in the same hours, taking red eyes to New York to work all day and catch a flight back that night, only to start again the next day somewhere else. We weren't in startup mode; we were in survival mode and the objective was the same: Cash Flow.

As there is in entrepreneurial startups, there were sales to manage, accounting to get done, vendors to pacify, reps to inspire, personnel to manage.

The biggest difference and this is major, is that running another company, regardless of the issues, does have existing cash flow and a basic infrastructure. Starting with something is better than starting with nothing.

Control of Vision

I believe that any venture requires a vision. And I really do mean a vision—that somewhere out on the horizon you see a

59

destination. It has form and structure and color and you "see" it clearly and want to get there regardless of the obstacles.

When I was CEO, I had a vision of what I wanted the company to be. I saw it clearly and, while I didn't know how to get there, I knew we would if we kept moving forward. What I didn't anticipate was that as I got closer and closer to my vision, we were getting farther and farther from the founder's vision. That's a big problem. And while we worked to adapt and find commonality, eventually it became a point of friction. And as we often said behind closed doors, "The battle is out there, not in here."

Owning your own company allows you control over your vision. However, this can be a great illusion. As CEOs or entrepreneurs you can delude yourself into believing that you are in control. The customer is in control and she can decide to fire you at any time by simply not purchasing your product.

To adequately influence your vision you must ensure that it agrees with and delivers on the needs and wants of your market. Otherwise you can have your vision but the customers who carry you to the destination will leave and you'll be left with a gulf too impossibly wide to cross on your own. So, you can be your own boss, but remember who the boss really is.

Immediacy

Entrepreneurs, business managers, CEOs, etc., are not patient people. We want it yesterday. One of the most interesting aspects of running my own company is the immediacy with which I can create positive change. If I want a contract written, I write it. If I want a book acquired, I acquire it. If I want a new webpage created, I create it. If I want a book edited differently, I edit it. If I want a distribution partner, I call them. If I want a different printer, I contact them. The only bureaucracy I have is how to manage all the things I want to get done in one day.

When I was CEO, we focused on the principle of multiplying the work we do. The idea was to set objectives and delegate to accomplish significantly more than one person can accomplish on his own. This works really well when everyone is tuned to the same notes, all are reading the same score, everyone is playing in tune, and what you play sells tickets. But managing that symphony can often lead to "Concordia discors" and nothing gets done or it takes way too long. I am convinced that most companies run way too fast and that rather than becoming more organized, companies allow entropy to enter and slow their mission. Having a very young and nimble company me to pivot quickly and get it done now rather than wait for the meeting, discussion, or handwringing to end.

At some point I'm either going to burn out or get more help. At that point the objective will be to maintain the entrepreneurial, full-speed mentality, but with better systems to protect the organization. I've seen it done.

Risk versus Reward

Some people believe that there is little risk to working for someone else. I think that is another delusion. There is always risk. You can be fired, laid off, outsourced, the company can intend to transition but doesn't, the company can be sold, the market can shift . . . Risk is inherent in life.

As for rewards, working for someone else has a tremendous reward in that you can focus on a specific job, believing that everyone else who works there is also focusing on their job, making the entire organization functional. I believe that the definition of teamwork is individuals executing assigned responsibility. There is great reward for working at an organization where such is the case. We can have many benefits beyond our paycheck including less stress and peace of mind.

Working for myself has forced on me a much greater appreciation for all those people I worked with who helped the company succeed. I appreciate the editors for their copywriting skills, the publicity department for their phone calls and emails, the receptionist who screened calls and kept paper in the copier. You get the idea. Working for yourself wakes you up to the realization that a company is dependent on the skills of many.

While the obvious rewards include getting to choose the eighty hours you work each week and making millions of dollars when you cash out, the reality is that most people, particularly book publishers, don't start companies to sell them. They create them because they want to create. And as for the millions, it's possible but not likely.

Education

This was unexpected, but I have learned more about publishing, technology, my own capacity, and business this year than I learned in the previous five years. Having an unintended consequence of my venture be knowledge and growth is a fantastic benefit to owning one's own company. Publishers are curious people and being part of a larger organization can sometimes, if we let it as I did, reduce our opportunity for growth. I remember the first time I figured out how to grab a script and import it into InDesign so that I could create an automatic index based on some key words. I was as excited as a little kid. And when I figured out how to create wireframes for websites I thought I was the cat's meow. I've been excited to learn that there's a lot more fun in business than reading pro formas, talking with business partners, and creating a partnership. I've rediscovered my love of learning.

Impact on Family

I came at this venture believing that I'd be able to manage the business and the family and not let either get in the way. I was wrong. Entrepreneurship can, at times, be overwhelming as a book must get to the printer on that day or that file must be uploaded then or that partner must hear back from us immediately. This has an impact on family in that there is no one else to delegate to. My wife, after spending the last twenty years raising children, is involved and that's exciting for both of us. Working with your spouse has its own advantages and disadvantages, but that's for a different article. Recently, one of my sons said that I should find some more money so "Mom wouldn't have to be at the computer." Ouch!

I have to make choices each day that determine what is more important—the business or the family. In the end, the family has to win because the enterprise is a means not an end. My family and I have had to talk through issues, where we invite the entire family in and counsel together about how to manage the business and the family. Understanding that it's not perfect and that the family is the first priority is helpful. I have to temper my enthusiasm and not believe that I'm championing some all-important cause. It's a means. It's a means. It's a means . . .

Conclusion

So, is being an entrepreneur or intrepreneur better? Yes, they both are great and have different benefits. I'm fortunate in that I've had both experiences. I'm more appreciative and inspired by those who launch companies and succeed. And I'm more appreciative of those who make existing companies succeed. What I've learned through both experiences is that action is better than inaction. Decide and move forward. Put one foot in front of another and don't fear taking that next step. While the vision is there and is a destination, the journey is also the destination.

# Ambition That Defined Ambition: The Restaurant Business

*The Marc Renson Turnaround Story*

Ambition Bistro

www.ambitionbistro.com

Why did I start you ask? I started my restaurant (Ambition) simply because I wanted to own a restaurant. No other reason. I had an idea of what I wanted to serve, I saw the Hollywood atmosphere in my mind and the idea of playing all the pop music of the 80's tickled me to death! I was 29 years old when Ambition opened its doors.

Who supported me? My partner who is also the co-owner, constantly reinforced positive thoughts in my mind reminding me of the wonderful things I would do and was doing, connecting and sharing my restaurant with friends unknown, building community trust, respect and a loyal following. We received loans from our local government, and finally of course, my family.

Any doubts? Everyday! There is that little thing called The Recession. Snowy days, hurricanes, beautiful 80 degree days, other restaurants that open up, competition, TAXES, upkeep on an old building, employee theft, equipment failures, lawsuits, insurances...did I miss anything? It all leads to me saying is this really worth it? But the answer has always been yes! I love what I do and wouldn't trade it for anything.

The highs. Realizing the law of attraction really does work. I love food, music and Hollywood. And all of that is what Ambition is. I'm nationally published. I feed celebrities who appreciate me and I'm able to share my dream with all who enter. Making people smile, meeting repeat customers and watching their children grow, touching lives, sharing my customers' successes. Most importantly, feeling appreciated is the most gratifying feeling of owning a restaurant. Customers who appreciate who we are and what we do.

The lows. Mostly only happens when the money runs out. Trusting employees/friends who stole money from my restaurant, people who think I'm rolling in dough and having to say no when they ask for donations. I'm really trying to think of the lows and it's hard. Because I choose not to remember the punches, I only choose to remember the success of winning the fight. And every day is a fight. Some days more than others. Everyday as I turn the key to lock the door, I always say thank you! After I fed ESPN founder Bill Rasmussen, he signed my poster "Ambition always wins!" I hold on to that in my darkest moments.

My restaurant just had a thirteenth anniversary and we received a Letter of Recognition and Congratulations from our NYS Governor Andrew Cuomo. I feed Hollywood celebrities. Bradley Cooper, George Hamilton, Ryan Gosling, Bethenny Frankel and many more!

# So Busy That I Had To Start My Own Business!

*The Stacy Kildal Turnaround Story*

Radio Free QuickBooks

www.radiofreeqb.com

Let's go back in time a bit, shall we? Specifically to the fall of 2001. I had just quit a job that I dearly loved due to some of the worst gender discrimination I've ever seen, and found out that I was pregnant. One of my friends that owned a plumbing company asked me to fill in at the office while his wife was on vacation. They were using QuickBooks 1998, which I'd worked in before, in older versions. Seeing the set-up and the mess that it was in, during the week that I was there, I completely cleaned it up. The millions in undeposited funds, the years of open invoices, the bank accounts that hadn't ever been reconciled. I was hired part time, and we continued using QuickBooks. I eventually moved to full time, and that's when I really dug deep into QuickBooks. I found the sample files and used them to click on every item on every menu to see what it did. I used the help menu. After a while, I had our QuickBooks workflow down to a science, complete with manuals that had walk-throughs for every task I did.

Then in 2004, my boss asked if I was interested in doing the bookkeeping for his cousin's son who was opening an auto repair shop. YES. So I had my first client, only at the time, I had no idea it would be my first client, and one that I would still have nine years later.

I started looking online and by dumb luck stumbled upon the ProAdvisor Program, since I really didn't know what I was looking for – training? More "side jobs?" It doesn't really matter. The point is that I found it. I borrowed the money from my mom (we were broke newlyweds with an almost 2 year-old) and joined the program. I took the test and got my first certification on QuickBooks 2004, then quickly did 2005 since it had just become available. I WAS ON MY WAY.

Through a combination of the Find A ProAdvisor database and me scouring want ads for part time bookkeepers, I was able to find more clients. And these clients were WONDERFUL. They understood that I still worked full time, that I could only meet with them after hours and on weekends. About a year into all of this, I formed an LLC. Shortly after that, I realized that I could actually make a living doing this QuickBooks stuff.

I wasn't just doing bookkeeping, I was cleaning up data files, I was setting people up and training them. The tipping point came when I got so busy that I wasn't getting home from work until 10-11p almost every night. It wasn't fair to my daughter or my husband, and it wasn't fair to keep asking my clients to work so late with me. Not quite earning from my clients as I was with my full time job, I knew I the only way to do it would be to quit working at the plumbing company.

My husband and I discussed it so many times before I made the decision, and it was one of the most difficult decisions I've ever had to make. Not because of the fear of losing the security of a full time job – it was telling my boss and his wife. Over the four years that I had worked for them, they were by far, the most gracious people I had ever worked with and I had grown very close to them and their two daughters.

Over the next few years, I applied to council (didn't get in). I found the Certified QuickBooks User program (in beta at the time) and took that exam. And I worked HARD. I looked online for ads for part time bookkeepers and had spreadsheets to show these employers how much money they could save by hiring me instead of an employee.

There were days that I had six appointments – and that was before I started working remotely. I was still getting home late, but not 11 pm late.

Without going into too much detail, over the past six years, I applied and auditioned for the Trainer and Writer Network (then called the Speaker's Bureau), I started teaching classes to new businesses at the local county offices, to students and a local community college and at local school districts through their continuing education departments. I was asked to work trade shows, was lucky to be asked to do webinars for QuickBooks launch tours, learned to love QuickBooks Online, found a voice to write courses and blog articles.

I met other amazing QuickBooks ProAdvisors: MB Raimondi, Laura Madiera, Christine Galli, Bryce Forney and most importantly, Dawn Brolin. Along with her and Intuit Product Specialist Woody Adams, we started our weekly online radio show/podcast, www.RadioFreeQB.com, and now have the opportunity to share our experiences with anyone that chooses to listen to us. It's a resource we created because Dawn and I didn't have anything like it when we started, so when Woody suggested it offhandedly during a conference call about a webinar, we jumped at it.

Without rambling on any longer, I guess I just want to say that because of the ProAdvisor program, I got a CAREER. A career that I absolutely love, with a community of professionals I respect and feel so lucky to be a part. But most of all, a career that affords me the luxury of taking my kids to school each morning, picking them up every day, and taking off a warm, sunny day in March to play in the backyard with them.

# How A Desire To Help Others Helped Start A Business

*The Hakan Mikado Turnaround Story*

Project Hawk

www.ProjectHawk.com

My name is Hakan Mikado, you can call me Hawk. I am the founder of Project Hawk and the creator of our "Vision to Strategies Formula™" and our "8 Point Business Success Blueprint™.". I would like to introduce myself first. I am from San Diego, and have our HQ just down the road from where I currently live in Mira Mesa. I personally love San Diego because there is such a large entrepreneurial spirit here.

I personally discovered my own entrepreneurial spirit when I was in Second Grade. I learned to sell paper balloons and fortune tellers, and was able to increase my profit margin by 400% within a year.

At the age of eight I had traveled the world four times and I learned how to make trinkets like bracelets and key-chains. I started off selling them for $10, then increased my prices to $40 average when I started using hemp and imported beads. So by the age of 10 I was making an average of $40 for every hour I worked. Granted, I only worked four hours per week.

The next year, I was assigned to create a business during a school project. I first created a business to teach people how to play D&D but no one wanted to learn. So after long though I had a brilliant idea to help other people start and grow their businesses. That was when Project Hawk was born. I helped other students complete projects, design plans, find tools, and I also worked in my family's businesses for the next seven years.

I was then introduced to drugs and alcohol and lost myself in a haze of abuse, one of the reasons I give back by helping addicts awaken their entrepreneurial spirit through a charity program. From 2007 to 2010, I worked in three corporate jobs and worked my way up from being entry level to a supervisor in six months average, but was not satisfied and worsened my abuse.

In 2010, I found my way out and aligned myself with my purpose in life. I hope that you will follow your own passion in life and accept your calling as a business person.

Once I had found my path again, I took my vision for the future and created a strategy to master it. I landed a huge project and a few other small projects along the way, so much to where I became comfortable. Nothing good comes from being comfortable, so when that huge project was coming to an end, I struggled to grow my company, I had no clients lined up, no current prospects, nothing in place, so I brought on four independent contractors, and then was let down. I ended up spending a lot of time and money trying to get them going only for them to give up.

Now at that point I had one project that was paying for the cost of doing business, just keeping the doors open, so I hit the streets, did lots of research, wrote a whole new plan, and fired everyone who worked with me. It was time to start over, and it was the best decision I could have made. I brought on three partners, three employees, and have another four being hired at the end of May when they finish school.

The next step in that process is to open the doors to entrepreneurs around the nation. We are opening up fifty-five offices around the US by August 28, 2014 and Project Hawk will be fully self-sustained by that point. According to the State of CA BOE (during a workshop I attended) If one in three businesses hired one person, we would have a 0% unemployment rate. Now I understand that this is difficult to do. So if I can encourage (by finding someone who can help them) just one in six businesses to hire one additional person through a growth strategy that will actually increase their profits, and help the other one in six (unemployed) people to start their own business, we would still have a 0% unemployment rate and a much wealthier nation overall.

I have a big vision and I want to share it with everyone, inspire people to do what they love, be the person they are meant to be, create the wealth they want for their family, have the time to spend with their community, and the freedom to do anything they want to do!

# A Dream Business That Reached Nearly $1m In Three Years

*The Crystal L Kendrick Turnaround Story*

The Voice Of Your Customer

www.thevoiceofyourcustomer.com

The Voice of Your Customer was founded in 2005, primarily as a secret shopping company designed to assist small businesses to improve customer service.

For my entire professional career, I aspired to become a Vice President of Customer Service for a Fortune 500 company. I earned an MBA in Management, accepted domestic and international assignments, and completed several management training courses.

As a hobby, I wrote articles for the local African American newspaper and completed secret shopping initiatives for friends who owned small retail establishments in the region. In 2007, I had the opportunity to expand my volunteer work into full time employment and with some fears, I transitioned my aspiration to excel in Corporate America to developing a nationally recognized minority and woman owned marketing firm. I applied for various business certifications, established a line of credit and identified several role models and mentors to assist with the launch process.

With the launch of The Voice of Your Customer, secret shopping

75

services expanded to include telephone/audio/video recordings, website assessments and observations of services provided by home improvement technicians, mechanics and other skilled tradespersons. The company also transitioned the secret shopping services to include audits, compliance, and product testing and expanded the client list to include non-profit organizations.

In addition, The Voice of Your Customer became a government contractor.

Today, The Voice of Your Customer is a full-service marketing firm that assists clients to penetrate niche markets using surveys, focus groups, secret shopping and media campaigns. Additional services include in-depth interviews, program and market assessments, discrimination testing, business training, public relations, and social marketing campaigns.

The firm is certified as a small, minority owned, woman owned and disadvantaged business. The firm serves a variety of clients as a Tier 1 and a Tier 2 supplier that include federal, state, regional, county and local governments; non-profit organizations; privately owned businesses; corporations; health care providers; and educational institutions. The firm is headquartered in the Walnut Hills community of Cincinnati, Ohio, with employees and subcontractors in the US, Latin America and Africa.

For outstanding achievements in performance, innovation and community involvement, The Voice of Your Customer has been recognized by the Cincinnati Chamber of Commerce, Ohio Civil Rights Commission, Public Relations Society of America – Cincinnati Chapter, South Central Ohio□Minority Supplier Development Council, US Small Business Administration, and Women's Business Enterprise – South East.

In 2009, The Voice of Your Customer was named the National Minority Supplier Development Council MBE of the Year for Sales Less than $1 million. In three short years, I achieved my goal of national recognition and achievements.

# Out Of A Near Death Experience A Business Is Born!

*The Kelli Minson Turnaround Story*

Gravity Solutions Inc.

www.Gravity1st.com

It was 4:00 in the morning when my husband Matt awakened me unable to speak. He held up a piece of paper with the words "Call 911" written on it. Because my husband is a physician and a first responder, my initial clouded thought was to ask him, "Is this a drill?" It wasn't a drill.

(In the last thirteen years, Dr. Matthew Minson (52) has responded to every major disaster in the U.S., including Ground Zero, as the Medical Director for Texas Task Force 1.)

In fact, Matt was suffocating...

As she dialed the phone Matt calmly jotted down a quick medical history for the paramedics should he be unconscious when they arrived. In the emergency department they were informed by the doctor that Matt's condition was an inflamed larynx, caused by Silent Reflux Disease. Matt had never experienced any of the typical signs or symptoms of Reflux until this near fatal episode.

According to the emergency doctor, Matt's esophagus was inflamed and very raw looking. The doctor explained it was a wonder that he had not died. When he was released they were told that Matt would have to take a very expensive prescription medication and that he must sleep with his head elevated in a straight line six to nine inches above his feet. Fortunately for her, the doctor overheard Kelli say "we can stop and buy a short wedge on the way home," and he immediately corrected her. Sleeping on a short wedge bends you in the middle of your body, making Reflux worse.

It puts added pressure on your LES (lower esophageal sphincter) it's the valve at the end of your esophagus that keeps everything in your stomach where it belongs – in your stomach. Sleeping head elevated without being bent in the middle proved to be quite a challenge. It was not as easy as it sounds Kelli explains "when we got home, I looked at our bed and decided that there were no wooden blocks or phone books that were going to elevate *this* bed, so I had to get inventive—literally."

Kelli experimented with everything trying to achieve the Doctor recommended position of head elevated sleeping: piled pillows, bolstering wedges, using a recliner, but nothing allowed Kelli's husband to achieve the rest he so desperately needed to feel better. Had she not listened to the doctors' words, "Head elevated in a straight line," she would not have begun constructing her own head elevated sleeping surface for Matt.

This was my first prototype Kelli explains—it was constructed from a rolled up rug with two metal shelves placed on an incline and our inflatable camping mattress. I called it my CostCo prototype because everything came from CostCo. This elevated Matt to the recommended height and allowed him to sleep in any position, unlike a short foam wedge, which according to the doctor "forces you to sleep on your back and can make reflux worse".

Matt slept here for eight weeks, letting his esophagus heal from the constant assault from stomach acid that he used to experience while sleeping on a flat surface. It looks funny, but it worked. It was just the right incline and he slept symptom free.

Every morning while Matt was upstairs getting ready for work, I would sit in the kitchen looking at my CostCo incline sleeping arrangement on the living room floor. I kept thinking to myself "if that inflatable mattress were shaped like a wedge of cheese, and if it were king sized, we could just put it on top of our own bed." Kelli explains, "I always tell people that the incline was for Matt—the fact that it disappears in the morning and I can make the bed normally, that was all for me. It also makes it easy to travel with."

After eight weeks of inclined sleeping, Matt and Kelli still had to return to the hospital for a biopsy to make sure Matt did not have Barrett's Esophagus or worse, esophageal cancer.

While they waited for the results of his biopsy, Kelli listened as the doctor interviewed Matt regarding his family health history. She was stunned to learn that Matt's grandfather had died from esophageal cancer and she was now completely motivated by fear for her husband's life. "I started reading everything I could get my hands on; I even read Heartburn and Reflux for Dummies. But it was a Johns Hopkins Health Alert on Reflux that convinced me to develop and patent my idea," explains Kelli.

White Paper / Reflux : February 25th, 2008 Johns Hopkins

*Recent research suggests that some lifestyle changes are more helpful than others for treating the symptoms of GERD. Treating GERD is important. Untreated GERD can lead to serious complications, such as esophageal ulcers, esophageal strictures, Barrett's esophagus and esophageal cancer.*

Doctors often recommend *lifestyle changes* as the *first-line treatment* for GERD. Researchers looked at the results of 100 studies conducted on various lifestyle measures for GERD. *Only losing weight and elevating the head of the bed showed a clear benefit in well-designed studies.*

"After I read the Hopkins report, I knew I was doing everything I

79

could to keep Matt's reflux under control and that it was crucial for him to sleep on an incline in order to allow his esophagus to heal. After we got the good news that Matt did not have Barrett's or esophageal cancer, I took a deep breath and I sat down at my computer. I spent the next three days taking a tutorial on the United States Patent and Trademark office website on how to write and file your own patent and a few days later, I did just that."

A little more than a year later, her first patent was issued. "I remember calling the CEO of an inflatable mattress company at 10:00 on a Saturday morning," Kelli said, "and he actually answered the phone." I simply said "Sir, you don't know me, you've never heard my name, I'm just a girl who has a good idea and if you will give me fifteen minutes of your time, I think you will be glad that you did."

Not only did he give her fifteen minutes, he offered her a licensing agreement with a nationally known producer of inflatable products. They began research and development of her idea, taking it from paper to product and The Gravity1st ™ elevated sleep systems mattress was born. "It was incredible," Kelli remembers, "sitting at the board room table with nineteen people at my first presentation and every other person in the room either had reflux, was married to someone who had reflux or knew someone who had died from esophageal cancer." My story resonated with them – if it could happen to a doctor, it could happen to anyone.

The mattress allows the linear drop necessary for anyone who requires the aid of gravity to rest and allows him or her to sleep on their back, side or stomach.

As the owner and CEO of Gravity Solutions, LLC, Kelli launched her product on her website Gravity1st.com and soon after was contacted by SkyMall catalog and invited to appear on their New Inventors Showcase page. Recently her company partnered with ECAN.org (Esophageal Cancer Action Network), RefluxMD.com and TreatBarretts.com.

Together we are trying to educate people about the dangers of heartburn, reflux and esophageal cancer. A nationwide campaign by ECAN to bring awareness to Esophageal Cancer Awareness Month (April), asking each individual state to issue a proclamation was launched and Kelli got right to work. Not only did she manage to get a proclamation from the Governor of the State of Texas, she took it a step further and made a request of the City of Houston for a proclamation as well. They were presented by Mayor Annise Parker at a public session of City Council on March 26, 2013. In February, in preparation for National Esophageal Cancer Awareness month, Treat Barrett's .com launched a nationwide ad campaign featuring Dick Smothers (remember him from The Smothers Brothers?). The commercials are leading up to the April Awareness Month and fund raising events for esophageal cancer research.

"It's a big job and I never imagined that a trip to the emergency room would turn into a business or that I would be starting a second career at the age of 51, but here I am. I love hearing from people who have tried Gravity1st and I enjoy knowing that we have helped to improve their lives.

"The response has been overwhelming; even more so now that our near tragedy has been turned into something that is helping so many people. They say that necessity is the mother of all invention and in our case it could not have been more accurate."

# If You Can't Find A Job, Make One!

*The Shaun Walker and Reid Stone Turnaround Story*

HERO|farm

www.hero-farm.com

How I Got Started:

In March of 2007, I was hired by an ad agency after interning for them for six months, where I worked until being let go in November 2008.

A co-worker from that agency and I worked together for about a year and a half before being laid off during the height of the recession. Of course, whenever a recession happens, the first budget to be slashed is marketing. We felt the period's effects far sooner than most.

Once laid off, we interviewed for a few available jobs, but no one was truly hiring – especially in our industry. We figured that if no one was going to give us a job, we may as well make some ourselves. It was at this point that we decided to combine our talents – I was a creative and he was in account management – and started HERO|farm in late 2008, a venture with a social mission and new thinking in mind for the ad industry. Just recently, numerous national articles describing similar situations for other members in the ad industry have been written.

Another company, led by individuals who are twice our age, is doing what HERO|farm began doing two years ago. Our model is revolutionary for the "dying" and fragmented ad industry, which is suffering tremendously still.

We also utilized our connections to start up with some clients and hired several other former co-workers who had also been laid off, using them as our contract workers.

Best Success Story:

We thoroughly enjoy the success of one of our clients, myPhoneMD, a smartphone repair & accessory company based in Louisiana that has been a vital partner since initial brand development in 2009.

In less than a year, myPhoneMD has expanded from two locations in Mandeville and Baton Rouge to include four other stores in Baton Rouge, Lafayette, New Orleans and Charleston, South Carolina – with plans to grow even further nationally. Within the next twelve months, another ten stores will be opened.

Biggest Startup Challenge:

Consistency. Working in the advertising industry, especially during this economy, is tough. Companies, outside of mega brands like Coke, do not sign long-term contracts. Most jobs are on a project-to-project basis, which makes bringing in steady money difficult. This is a major challenge, although we have faced and continue to face several others.

#1 Tip for New Entrepreneurs:

Why wait for time when all it does is run? Whatever it is, do it and don't look back.

*Used by permission from YFS Magazine*

# Conclusion

Although I have been in business for many years and have helped a number of people establish themselves, I was very impressed by the stories I have included in this book. It is impossible to read them and not be encouraged inspired and uplifted to continue the pursuit of one's dream.

I have made seven observations about the story:

1.    Success in business has nothing to do with gender. It is evident that both males and females have the same business abilities and are capable of creating opportunities out of "nothing."

2.    The same struggles that keep other people in dead jobs were used by these people as a springboard for success. As I read the stories in this book, I could not help thinking about the reasons people have given me for not starting their own businesses. In compiling this book, I learned that the way we perceive our situation is what is important and not the situation itself.

3.    There are still great opportunities in this economic situation. It will shock you how many people have given up, hung up the books and gone into depression because of the economic situation of the world. What is a fact is that many people are building great businesses today more than ever before. The economic situation has single-handedly brought out the entrepreneurial spirit in many, including those in this book.

4.    Never give up your dream. The law of attraction and the result of persistence which worked for many of the entrepreneurs in this book, will certainly work for anyone who will not give up on their dreams. There is a saying that many great ideas go down

to the grave with people who should have executed them. That should never be said of us. We must die empty. If we do not give up on our dreams, what and who we need will be attracted to us to ensure the actualization of our dominant thoughts.

5.      Your business idea is needed. Included in these stories are businesses that save lives, some help save money; some provide longevity and some make people feel better about themselves. What happens when businesses are not set up is that many people suffer as a result. Both the person who refuses to start and those who would have benefited as a result, suffer as a result of inactivity. Are people suffering or even dying because you have refused to start your business? It is time to change!

6.      You have what it takes. It is a real shame that one of the strongest barriers preventing people from starting in business is the feeling of inadequacy. The "I don't have everything I need" feeling. I have always said to people that when you start your business, you don't know everything, your product is not perfect, you might not even be in the perfect market for you. All that is not a problem.

It is your desire to learn and your flexibility to change/tweak as you journey, that will allow you run a successful business. The reason people in these stories are successful is because they dared to start. Are you going to dare to start?

7.      You already have an idea. Many people are waiting for an idea or an a-ha moment. Honestly, all of us must have had an a-ha moment but maybe we did nothing with it or we thought that it must be rubbish. You don't need any more ideas; start with that one and grow your own successful business.

I want to challenge every reader who wants to start a business to simply get on with it and not delay any longer.

I also want to invite you to our FREE "Turnaround Webinars" where you get to hear the full story of each of the entrepreneurs featured in this book. Register now – by sending "register me" to admin@startyourownbusinessacademy.com.

# Free Bonus ···

FREE Bonus –

"How To Start Your Own Business In 30 Days"

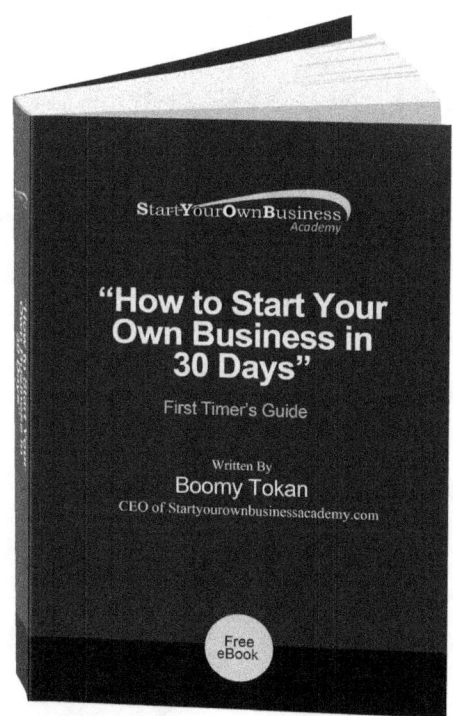

Hey … If you would like to learn how to start and run a "High Performance" business; then download this FREE guide. It will also show you how to start making money from your business within 30 Days! **Available only for a Limited Period.**

Click this link:

"How To Start Your Own Business In 30 Days"

Or Copy and paste in your browser:

http://startyourownbusinessacademy.com/free-bonus-download/

Enjoy

# Other Books By The Author

How To Write Your First Business Plan: With Outline and
Templates Book

(Includes USA-friendly content, plus the principles taught in this
book are transferable to any country.) Whenever the words
"Business Plan" are mentioned, most people freeze! What follows
are the words "I don't know how to write one."

In reality it need not be this way. That is why I have taken the lid
off and written in plain English what needs to be considered and
included within a business plan. This book has been written to
help those who are writing plans for the first time or for those who
write business plans infrequently. (Even seasoned business plan

writers will learn one or two things, I promise!) Finally, I have included my personal email for those who need further assistance. This service will be offered FREE for now.

Book Title: How To Raise Money For Your Business: The Ultimate Guide For Start Up Businesses; Book

If you want to know the truth about raising money for your business this book is for you.

If you are having a tough time raising the money you want for your business this book is for you too.

If you are not sure where to go to get the kind of funding you need for your business this book is just what you need.

After many years of helping businesses of various kinds raise the money they want, I have laid out in print all that you need to know about raising money for your start-up business! .

www.ingramcontent.com/pod-product-compliance
Lightning Source LLC
Chambersburg PA
CBHW051345170526
45166CB00002B/962